The Empty Nest Symphony

Mary McBride

with
Veronica McBride

To Sylvia and Larry Enjoy! Mary McBride

Illustrations by Christine Tripp

Published by BROTHERS GRIN PUBLISHING

Dedication

To my father, who taught me laughter is an important ingredient to happiness.

Library of Congress Cataloging in Publication Data

McBride, Mary
    The empty nest symphony/Mary McBride with Veronica McBride.
    1. Middle age—Humor.   I. McBride, Veronica.   II. Title.
PN6231.M47M36   1989 818'.5402—dc19   88-31821
ISBN 0-9627601-3-7

Edited by Bruce Lansky and Ellen Hawley
Illustrated by Christine Tripp
Production Editor: Sandy McCullough
Art Director: Kelly Nugent
Assistant Art Director: Shelagh Geraghty
Production Manager: Pam Scheunemann

92 5 4 3 2
Printed in the United States of America

Contents

Part 1
The Empty Nest

Chapter 1

It's Time to Take the Children's Number out of the Phone Book

Though it's your alma mater
There's an urge you'd better quell
When you're with your son on campus
Don't shout out the old school yell.

You hardly get the final payment made on the addition you built to make room for the kids and the kids leave home.. in this case it will be a son going off to college.

Sons have always left home and mothers have always cried. Nowadays, however, instead of going to the sugar bowl to get money for your son, you find your purse and hand over your credit cards.

You are never ready for the farewell. He still seems like a little boy. You think that the first thing he'll do when he gets to college is run up and down the corridors.

But going to college means he is grown up so you might as well start treating him as an adult. You'll avoid arguments if you follow this advice:

- Don't send him bunny- or Santa-shaped cookies.

- Don't teach his roommate how to take his temperature.

- Don't go through his clothes and mend them. He likes rips.

- Don't give him advice he'll just forget. Plan to send him pertinent Ann Landers columns.

- Don't call him at his dorm. If he isn't there, you'll worry something has happened to him. If he is there, you'll worry that he doesn't have any friends.

You may worry that partying will interfere with your son's getting through college...particularly if.

- He picked the college by the looks of the girls on the brochure.

- He has a beer-bottle opener on his key ring.

- He packs five Frisbees®

- His license plate says "STUD I."

- His major is "his little secret."

Before he leaves, here's a checklist that will make his departure less of a problem for you:

- Have him adjust the lawn mower down to its shortest cut so you won't have to mow as often.

- Make sure he has picked up all his wet towels.

- Have him look for library books he may have forgotten to return.

- Check to see that all your hard-to-open pill bottles are opened.

Your son will be lost in college without your sage advice.

- Have him notify all his friends who call in the middle of the night that he will no longer be home.

Now is your time of freedom. Don't spoil it by worrying about your son. Once you have done everything for him that a mother is expected to do, your feelings of concern should gradually die down. So be sure to give him your best advice:

- Make sure he can find his way to the library.

- Tell him to date only girls who can type.

- Let him know that one semester of college does not a résumé make.

- Change the saying about "All work and no play" to:

"All play and no work
Makes Jack a lazy jerk."

- Eavesdrop on other mothers giving advice to find out if you've forgotten anything.

- Then, after your final words of wisdom, have a basket of fruit delivered to his dorm room. It may be the only non-junk food he will eat until Thanksgiving.

Once he has left to start a new life, the best way for you to avoid empty-nest depression is to keep busy. Here's a list of things you can do the first day he is gone:

- Draw a beard on his high school graduation picture so you'll recognize him when you see him again.

- Write a letter of apology to his roommate.

- Divide your recipes by 3/4. (He ate over half of everything.)

- Cancel your book club membership. You'll no longer have to stay up late reading until he gets home.

- Take out a subscription to *TV Guide*. Now you'll be able to watch programs of your choice.

- Go out and buy a step stool. He'll no longer be there to reach items on high shelves.

When children leave home, parents enter a new phase of life. Try to enjoy it, even though there will be a few unpleasant surprises...like finding out it wasn't the children who left the cap off the toothpaste all those years—it was your husband.

Chapter 2

Sugar 'n Spice,
I Can't Wait
'til the Rice

There'll never be a time
When you feel more harried
Than the weeks before
Your daughter gets married.

A common way of emptying the nest is having a daughter get married. This is an expensive and nerve-wracking experience.

Matrimony has changed a lot since you got married—couples live together before the wedding and women keep their own name. Unfortunately, what hasn't changed is that the bride's parents cover the costs of the festivities. And your daughter is sure to be the type who wants a limo rather than a ladder. In fact, if you hold planning sessions to cut the wedding costs, each session will give you a higher total. One mother had to leave the wedding reception early to go to the job she took to help pay for the wedding.

But a bigger problem than the cost of the festivities is trying to coexist with your daughter until the wedding. She'll get testier every day—at the fifth fitting she might decide she hates the dress—and she's too old for you to tell her that Santa's watching.

7

She'll pick up on everything, saying things like, "The less it costs the more you 'ooh' and 'aah.'" And she'll be against anything you suggest. If you say, "How about pink mints?" she'll want white, green or yellow.

One mother became so worn-out shopping for the wedding dress that when her daughter couldn't decide between two she said, "Well, take *both.*"

All daughters have their own ideas, and they get really stubborn about them at this time. One bride who was a vegetarian wanted the guests to throw brown rice. One wanted the "Just Married" sign to be in calligraphy. Another young bride insisted that her "something blue" be her jeans.

Of course, you'll buy at least one book detailing wedding preparations, but the following helpful hints may not be included:

- Practice writing like your daughter so if six months have gone by and she hasn't written her thank-you notes, you can do it.

- Spend at least fifteen minutes a day working on the guest list. You can't invite someone by phone on the day of the wedding, telling her everyone is being invited that way.

- Don't print the Surgeon General's warning about smoking on the matchbook covers. The bride and groom's names are enough.

- When you pick the color of your dress, bear in mind that your hair will be grayer by the wedding day.

- Don't hum the wedding march as a hint that your daughter should be working on the wedding.

- Don't put finding a reception hall on the list of last-minute details.

Everyone thinks a mother feels bad about losing a daughter. She's expected to cry at the wedding. But, since the mother's been living through at least ten outbursts a day, it stands to reason that the emotion she'll feel at the wedding won't be sadness. But you don't want to be the one mother who proves everyone else wrong, so try hard to look sad:

- Have an onion worked into your corsage.

- Smudge some mascara on your cheek to make it look like you've been crying.

- Wear a too-tight girdle.

- Wear shoes that hurt.

Even more important than trying to look unhappy is trying not to look elated.

- Don't draw smile faces on the invitations.

- Don't pump the groom's arm excessively after the ceremony.

Carrying the bride's bags to the car is not proper etiquette.

- Don't use noisemakers after the "I dos."

- Above all, remember that it is not proper etiquette for the mother of the bride to carry the bride's bags to the car.

With all the money and emotion that go into the event, it's too bad there isn't a column in the guest book labeled "Remarks," where people could write rave reviews.

Chapter 3

Fighting over the Check Burns Calories

When the first course has ended
Do they have to bring the cart?
"No, thank you" comes much harder
If you see each cake and tart.

When kids stop spilling milk, they start ordering steak, so eating out with a family gets awfully expensive. But once the kids are gone, you can start going out for meals again. The most important consideration is to try to find a restaurant whose food is least likely to wake you up at 2 A.M.

If it's been a long time since you've eaten out, you should review restaurant etiquette. For instance, don't worry if you see a sign that says "We Do Not Serve Barefoot Customers," you can still slip off your shoes under the table if your corns hurt. Here are some more dos and don'ts:

- Make reservations in just one name. The others in your group won't be offended. And when you make your reservations, you don't have to tell what you'll be wearing when you come in.

- If you take a table in the smoking section because there are no vacant tables in nonsmoking, don't lecture the smokers about smoking.

- Don't say, "I was here first!" if someone is waited on ahead of you. They're apt to say, "Were you ever!!"

- Don't say, "Is there a doctor in the house?" and then ask him or her to order for you.

- When the waitress says, "My name is Shirley and I'm your waitress," you don't have to introduce yourself and everyone else at the table to her.

- If you get lonely eating by yourself, "crash" another group by saying, "If I join you I'll bet I could get your little boy to eat his peas."

- If your napkin falls on the floor, don't use the napkin from under the dinner rolls.

- You don't have to tip the waitress again if she runs after you with your doggy bag.

One last bit of advice: if the restaurant is so dark you can't read the menu, just excuse yourself and take it into the restroom.

If you're lonely, join a group

Chapter 4

If You Have Trouble Climbing Stairs, Don't Take up Mountain Climbing

Though skiing is quite trendy
It's a sport you'd better dodge.
It'll be a lot less risky
Just sitting in the lodge.

Now that your children have moved out, you'll have much more freedom. This is the time to devote yourself seriously to your hobby or to start a new hobby if you've never had one.

Not just any hobby will do. For instance, trying all thirty-one flavors at Baskin-Robbins is not a good hobby. Neither is eating at every fast-food restaurant in town. Here are some more hobby selection "don'ts."

- Your hobby shouldn't produce anything your children will fight over after you are gone.

- Don't pick a hobby you have to clean up after.

- Don't grow flowers if it means your husband will stop sending them to you.

Make sure to select a hobby that is not harmful to your health.

- Don't take up bird-watching or your husband might use the binoculars to look in the neighbors' windows.

- Don't get started on crossword puzzles because you'll be embarrassed to find your children and grandchildren know more words than you do.

One way to find a satisfying hobby is to read your high school reunion bulletin and see what your classmates' hobbies are. If nothing there appeals to you, brainstorm with a friend to come up with one.

Here are a few hobbies you might enjoy:

- Writing clever sayings for your answering machine. Try to make them so appealing that people will actually leave messages.

- Looking for people whose driver's license pictures are worse than yours.

- Looking for people who have more health problems than you.

- Juggling. (Practice only when a grandchild is there to pick things up.)

- Thinking up excuses for *not* baby-sitting.

- Shopping for presents at rummage sales. (It will hurt less when your presents aren't appreciated.)

- Finding new people to show your grandchildren's pictures to.

- Getting second, third and fourth opinions from doctors.

- Trying to detect who's had a face-lift.

- You could even make a hobby of thinking up hobbies.

People sometimes overdo hobbies. They get too many. One woman planted a garden and wove a basket before her morning golf game. Other people get carried away with a single hobby. You'll know you've gone too far with ceramics if people you've exchanged gifts with for years suggest you just exchange cards this year.

Chapter 5

Volunteer
for the Job of Saying,
"Keep Your Fork"

Nothing's better than to know
That people have been fed
But don't be spreading gossip
While grace is being said.

Many women get more involved in church and synagogue activities once their children leave home. Dinners have to be put on and members of the congregation must come forward to do the work.

It's easy to think of reasons you shouldn't volunteer. For example, you could spill hot coffee on someone and be sued. However, doing your duty at these events will bring you a lot of enjoyment.

Remember that kitchen crews have unwritten rules. Don't bow from the waist when you're called out to be recognized. And don't stand in the corner reading the church bulletin while everyone else is working.

To make yourself a popular worker:

● Don't suggest chips when everyone's trying to decide what kind of potatoes to serve.

- Don't wear your fuzzy bedroom slippers, no matter how much your feet hurt.

- Don't complain that your dishtowel is wet—just keep drying.

- Don't hang around the buffet table waiting to over-hear a compliment on something you brought.

- Don't yell, "If everyone would take their dishes to the sink and rinse them it would sure help."

Your assistance will also be welcomed at bazaars, but remember to sit on the folding chair provided for you—don't bring your recliner from home.

A few more tips for bazaars:

- Don't wear a change apron if you don't want to remain standing.

- Contribute something unique so it can't be com-pared to what someone else brought.

- Don't force your recipe on the people who buy your cookies. If they want it, they'll ask for it.

- Don't set your table up in the hall to catch people on the way in.

- Don't volunteer to work at games if you're a softie—you're apt to give prizes to every child who cries.

- If you decide to bring your husband's tackle box to hold money, make sure it isn't fishing season.

Singing in a choir also benefits others and brings enjoy-ment to you. Unfortunately, not everyone who joins the choir has a beautiful voice. Many people join because they think they look good in a choir robe. Here's how to tell if your singing talents aren't fully appreciated:

Watch for signs that your musical talent is not fully appreciated.

- There's not enough choir music to go around, and you're always the one who's left shorthanded.

- You're handed a list of other volunteer jobs.

- You're asked to sing from the cry room.

- Someone tells you that your family misses having you sit with them during the service.

- When you ask what page the hymn is on, people refuse to tell you.

- You are asked to lip sync.

Bear in mind that your help will be appreciated in many areas. Maybe your church or synagogue work should be teaching Sunday or Sabbath School. If you don't want to do it every week, volunteer to be a substitute, or maybe just a substitute for a substitute.

Chapter 6

I Only Clean During Commercials

I get great pleasure from my TV.
The stars give me a thrill.
It almost makes me feel guilty
That they're missing from my will.

Honest people will tell you, "To me, a great time is eating a TV dinner on a TV tray in front of the TV." And when the kids leave home, you can finally watch TV to your heart's content.

Too many people think they should act as if they hate television, when in reality it's the most pleasure-giving invention of modern times. Those people say things like, "I don't even know why we own the dumb thing," or "I just turn it on to have voices in the house."

But women who have a healthy respect for television are often more forthright about their sentiments:

- "Even when it was just wrestling and Uncle Miltie, I chose TV over my husband."

- "I'm never anxious for my grandchildren to learn to walk. When they're still crawling they're not blocking the TV screen."

- "I vote for the candidate who talks fastest so they'll get back to regular programming sooner."

- "I got stuck at the doctor's office, so I called a friend from the clinic and she put the phone up to her TV.

- "Any minister who quotes something he heard on TV has my attention."

- "I pride myself on being able to spot a rerun within the first ten seconds."

- "It's so nice that my grandchildren are getting married on Saturday when TV is mainly cartoons."

- "Some people quote Shakespeare. I quote Blanche on 'Golden Girls'."

- "My quilt pattern is the TV test pattern."

- "The only reason I shovel the walk is so the mailman can deliver my *TV Guide*."

If you're one of those meek souls who gets intimidated by the people who look down on TV watchers, here's an ample supply of impressive sounding reasons for watching TV:

- "It's a great way to keep up with the latest fashions."

- "I get lots of exercise racing around during commercials."

- "I keep it on to ward off burglars."

- "Disagreeing with the guests on talk shows gets my blood moving."

You shouldn't for a minute be apologetic about watching TV, but you might be interested to find out whether you're a TV addict. Here's how you can tell you're hooked on TV:

- The only cause you were ever involved in was bringing back a TV show.

- Names you suggest for grandchildren always come from TV characters.

- You hum TV theme songs.

- The only item you have engraved for identification in case of theft is your television set.

- Instead of calling your children when the rates are low, you call during dull TV times.

- While you read a book, you think about how it could be turned into a TV miniseries.

- You have your TV repair person's phone number programmed for automatic dialing.

Still, no matter how great something is, it can always be better. The suggestions which follow could help you enjoy television even more:

- Teach your dog to growl when a grandchild tries to change the channel you are watching.

- Leave your Halloween treats in a bowl on the front steps while you watch TV in peace.

- When the phone rings, turn the television up so the caller knows she's interrupting your viewing.

- Keep a list of which friends watch which shows so you'll know who to call if you doze off before your show ends.

You do have to be careful about TV, however. If you have a TV set in the kitchen, don't watch it when you're slicing, chopping or peeling.

Watching TV can be hazardous to your health.

Chapter 7

Clock Watching Through Bifocals

Let's make a pact between us
As we toil for daily wages.
We'll talk about most everything,
But not discuss our ages.

After the children have left home, many women who stayed home to raise them go out and get jobs. If you're one of them, remember you're apt to be noticeably older than your co-workers.

Young people just out of school will think you're ancient. But don't get paranoid. Not everything they do is meant to poke fun at your age. One woman who'd just returned to work after twenty years as a housewife and mother thought her colleagues were sending her memos because they thought she was forgetful.

But even if you're not paranoid, many things will remind you that you're not young. For example:

- You're the only one in the carpool who is let out at the door.

- Someone volunteers to get you a treat out of the vending machine and asks, "What can you eat?"

It's easy to underestimate your co-worker's age.

- The person bringing the rolls for coffee says, "I picked out a prune Danish just for you."

- You're the only one not questioned about writing graffiti on the bathroom wall.

- You're the only one the boss didn't have to apologize to after the Christmas party.

Not only do you seem older to your co-workers than you really are, they seem younger to you than they really are. You may be underestimating their age too much if:

- You expect them to go out for recess instead of a coffee break.

- You have the urge to ask them, "What do you want to be when you grow up?"

- You think the company magazine should have a page for them to color.

- You wonder why they're not in school.

When you consider that some of your co-workers won't be having hot flashes until the year 2000, it can be upsetting. Fight these depressing thoughts and don't call attention to your age.

- Don't tell anyone you'd prefer Norman Rockwell pictures on the wall instead of abstract art.

- Don't get your prescription filled on your lunch hour.

- Don't take pills at the water cooler. Learn to swallow them dry.

- Don't assume that the man a woman is living with is her husband unless you've actually been to the wedding.

- Don't ask how last night's TV movie turned out— they'll guess that you fell asleep before it ended.

- Don't let your mouth hang open if someone says something shocking.

- Don't mention that your house and car are paid for.

Instead, to perk up your image, try these tips:

- Put a ski rack on your car.

- Order "extra hot" and "the works" when you go out to lunch.

- Take a book with you to the restroom so they'll think you're engrossed in a novel and never guess you're constipated.

Above all, don't be upset when someone says, "You're like a mother to me." Remember, they could have said, "You're like a grandmother to me."

Chapter 8

Just When You Get the Hang of It, It's Time to Hang It Up

Where's the paper? Where's the carbon?
What's that little thingamabob?
No one asks more questions
Than a temp with a brand-new job.

A temporary service is a great idea for the woman who wants to work but doesn't want to be tied down to a year-round, forty-hour-a-week job.

- You can get by with a small wardrobe because your clothes will always be new to your constantly changing co-workers.

- You can use your crumpled-up mistakes as stuffing for the packages you mail.

There are also disadvantages to being with a temporary service. You'll feel like an outsider. When everyone else is drinking coffee from their own mug, you will be drinking from a styrofoam cup. You'll always be the new kid on the block, so you'll have to be extra careful not to do anything offensive. For example:

- Don't ask work-related questions while people are on break.

- Park far, far away to be sure you aren't taking someone's parking space.

On the other hand, you shouldn't try too hard to get accepted. Don't try to find out about other workers just so you'll have gossip to add at the next coffee break. And, don't try to establish eye contact with the person looking over your shoulder. Above all, if you're asked to take drugs, don't feel you have to. Try responding with, "I would, but I'm just getting over the flu."

There are some other helpful hints for temporary workers that you should know about:

- Buy a large purse so you can hide your mistakes.

- Laugh not only at the boss's jokes but at the jokes of the person training you.

- If you only get one perfect letter done all day, be sure there's a stamp on the envelope when it's sent out.

- Remember that just dusting a computer the wrong way can wipe out a year's work.

- If your incompetence has lost a customer, don't try to make up for it by offering to buy whatever the customer was considering.

- Wear a pin that says "Temporary Services." People may be more patient.

- If they nickname you "Rusty," they're hinting that you need a refresher class in office procedures.

Remember that wearing a pencil behind your ear is no longer in vogue, and don't bring your 1962 manual typewriter with you. Never say, "What in blazes is that?" when you see an unfamiliar office machine.

Memorize these other taboos before you venture into the business world:

- Don't visit the person you're replacing to ask for help, especially if she's in the hospital.

Don't ask the person you replaced for help.

- Don't put the initials of the person you're replacing at the bottom of a letter just because you don't want to be blamed for it.

- Don't hang a "Do Not Disturb" sign on your office door.

- Don't use excuses like, "The fumes from the correction fluid affected my brain."

- Don't put letters to your children in the outgoing mail.

- Don't call the person you're replacing and beg her to take more time off because you're just starting to catch on.

When you get to work on the second day and see the boss at a typewriter, you'll know you aren't doing well. If afterwards, you get a thank-you note from the person you replaced, it may be just because her co-workers really appreciate her now.

Chapter 9

Overhead Puts You in over Your Head

You won't get rich in business
However hard you toil—
Unless you build your office
And under it find oil.

If you've ever said, "My dream is to have a business of my own," now is the time to make your dream come true.

Before you start, you'll want to learn what goes into running a business. There's more to it than receiving good luck floral arrangements, taking customers' money, and having business lunches. You'll work so many hours you'll have to ask a neighbor to take in your paper, feed your dog and water your plants.

To start a business, you need capital—a sizable amount—and offering a discount on your merchandise to the bank's loan officer will not guarantee that you get the loan. They'll want collateral, and the I.O.U.s that your kids put in your sugar bowl will not be enough.

One woman who was having difficulty getting financing said, "I thought I could write my memoirs to make money so I could finance a new business, but I realized I would have to have a successful business in order to write a memoir people would want to read."

A new venture is more likely to be a riches-to-rags than a rags-to-riches story. Even though you didn't intend to run a

Your kids' piggy bank won't impress your banker.

nonprofit business, it could easily turn out that way. You may get to the point where you consider selling your gold fillings.

The belief that you have to spend money to make money can ruin you. Don't put in a landing strip when a parking lot with a bicycle rack will do. But you *will* have to spend a lot of money to stay in business...especially for advertising. So, if you think of ways to get free advertising, use them, even if it means going to school for show-and-tell time or writing graffiti on restroom walls.

The following advice will help women starting a new business:

- Get into the habit of wearing sunglasses. When people ask you how your business is going and you say, "Great!" they won't be able to tell if you're lying or if you've been crying.

- Avoid family reunions. Family members expect to get things free.

30

- Dress for success. If you aren't sure what dress-for-success attire is, just buy clothes that say, "Dry Clean Only."

- Develop a firm handshake. You can practice this on the dog.

- Buy a deck of cards. You'll want to play solitaire while you wait for customers.

- Have a long spindle for your bills. The longer the spindle, the fewer the bills it will look like you have.

- Persevere. Don't have a going-out-of-business sale within a week of your grand opening.

Some sales methods are unacceptable. So, don't use them. Here are some definite no-no's:

- Getting down on your knees to a customer.

- Making a shopper give five good reasons why she won't buy the dress she tried on.

- Standing in front of your business and flagging people down.

- Putting an ad in the personals column saying, "Sharp business woman would like to meet customers."

No matter how bad things get, don't call up the people who said to "Go for it!" and tell them off. Instead, keep the following rules posted behind the cash register:

- It's all right to have humorous signs around like, "We Take Credit Cards, Cash or Bushels of Corn." However, customers may not take kindly to signs that say, "You Break Our Items—We Break Your Bones."

- You can entertain customers' children by having them play with the boxes in the storeroom, but don't lock the storeroom door.

- Be tactful when a customer's child is misbehaving. For example, you might say, "May I frisk your adorable little girl?"

Misery is watching a customer examine and reexamine an item as she gets into her car. Happiness is seeing someone drive up with a "Born to Shop" bumper sticker.

If all this seems overwhelming, maybe it would be better to forget going into business. Remember R-I-S-K is a four-letter word.

Chapter 10

Birthdays Occur Without Your Permission

You can't be blamed for thinking
That birthdays are a sin
If when you blow out candles
You must hold back your skin.

Why do people congratulate each other on birthdays when, for anyone over 39, birthdays are really misfortunes. Every birthday is an ugly reminder that you're getting older. That's why many people never pass their 39th birthday.

When you were a child and didn't need cheering up, you got pretty birthday cards with nice verses and money. Now, when you're sensitive about your age, you get cards that ridicule you for being old—and you're supposed to laugh. One "hilarious" birthday card read, "I'd like to get you a birthday drink," and inside it said, "How about some warm milk?" The next time you get an especially insulting birthday card, write a suicide note on it and return it to the sender!

When someone decides to throw a party in your honor it's even worse. How awful to be in a roomful of people who all know how old you are. And nowadays they videotape the whole

33

party and use the zoom lens for a close-up of your crow's feet.

Your birthday might be a little less painful if you consider these suggestions:

- Prepare a clever answer for the question, "How old are you?" Try, "Well, I no longer have to worry about zits."

- Don't eat Rice Krispies for breakfast. If the snap, crackle, pop seem fainter, you'll worry about your hearing.

- If you're given a gift with an inscription, don't read it out loud—you don't want anyone to see how bad your eyes are. Use the excuse that you don't want to cry in front of them.

Just remember that for several months you can pretend you aren't used to your new age, so, when asked, you can give your old age without really feeling that you're lying.

Save the video camera for your grandchildren's birthday.

Chapter 11

Don't Stick out Your Tongue When Your Doctor Puts You on a Special Diet

I'm on a special diet.
I admit I do feel better.
"My cholesterol is down"
Will be in my Christmas letter.

Why don't doctors ever say, "Try using a little more salt"? All their instructions tend to make life less pleasant. It doesn't matter how much you compliment their family pictures or ooh and aah over their diplomas; they'll get stricter and stricter as the years go on. It could help to have your colors done. You'll look healthier, and the doctor may not be as severe.

You might feel better about your doctor if you have a feast before each doctor's appointment. It may be the last time you are allowed to eat some of those foods.

It should make you feel better to know that aging brings restrictions into everyone's life. Some mid-lifers were heard to make these comments in a doctor's waiting room:

Succeeding on your new special diet takes a bit of creativity

- "Why is it that just as my eyes are starting to fail, I have to read the tiny print on all the packages?"

- "I hate to brag, but I still have my gallbladder."

- "Then I asked the doctor, 'Couldn't I give up nutmeg instead of salt?'"

- "Who looks healthy in an examination gown anyhow?"

- "So I asked him, 'Now is that one grain of salt per day or per week?'"

- "I wished he had asked me to give up sex instead of my favorite foods."

As dreary as your special diet may be, you must follow it. Here are a few suggestions to help:

- Dine only with other people on special diets.

- Shake an empty salt shaker over your food.

- If you're allowed only one cup of regular coffee, buy yourself a huge mug.

- Bring your own scale to the doctor's office.

You can't expect the doctor to cancel the special diet just because you offer to double your daily dosage of antacid tablets. Above all, don't throw the eggs you can't eat at your doctor's house on Halloween.

Chapter 12

Would You Please Take off Your "Thank You for Not Smoking" Button and Bring Me an Ashtray

Smoking made your clothes smell bad
Before you had to quit.
Now your clothes smell really fresh—
If only they would fit.

Doctors who will overlook your smoking are getting harder and harder to find, so you can expect that you'll eventually be told to quit. Nothing is more difficult than trying to stifle your smoker's cough in a doctor's office.

People who smoke invariably fight their physician's order to stop. They say outlandish things like, "I'm only smoking because people say there's nothing worse than a reformed smoker," or "I have to smoke for two now. My husband gave it up."

It's not that smokers aren't health conscious. Many of them choose the brand with the smallest warning on the package.

If you choose to give up smoking:

- Avoid actions that will make you want to smoke— like getting out of bed.

- Take up swimming—you can't smoke in the water.

- Don't keep matches around, not even for lighting birthday candles.

- If you used to enjoy lingering over a cigarette after eating out, dine with boring people so you'll want to go home.

It's understandable that you want to hang onto your beloved, though dangerous, habit for as long as possible. But don't ask the doctor for a light while he's advising you to give up cigarettes.

You will need a powerful excuse to combat your physician's orders.

Chapter 13

Pretend You Pump Iron Instead of Take Iron

When you buy something youthful
To give yourself a lift,
The clerk always asks,
"Shall I wrap it as a gift?"

If you're lucky enough to live out the normal life span, the term "old" will, at some point, apply to you. However, every woman struggles to stay young. One woman found out what scent her granddaughter wore and bought some for herself. But don't try this if your granddaughter is under two and smells like talcum powder.

To appear a bit younger than you are, try some of these suggestions:

- Hang a "hunk" calendar where visitors will see it.

- Keep a do-it-yourself manual on the coffee table, as if you really do fix things.

- Help your grandson deliver papers by bike, but don't ride a three-wheeler.

- Leave a blow-dryer lying around.

Borrow your daughter's scent, not your granddaughter's.

- Always take the liberal view, except when you're on jury duty.

- Only admit to having aches and pains that young people also get. Headaches are fine. If you break your hip, call it a broken leg.

- Sport a vanity license plate that says something like BABE or ZOOM.

- Lean on your horn if the person in front of you doesn't start up immediately when the light changes to green.

- Let everyone know about it if you get arrested for speeding.

- When you're caught napping, say, "I guess I shouldn't have stayed up so late reading *Cosmo*."

If you're going to avoid looking like an old-timer, study this list of "don'ts":

- Don't sit in a rocker with an afghan over your lap. One or the other is permissible, but not both.

- Don't let anyone know that the ancient date painted on the water tower was put there by your graduating class.

- Don't admit that you remember when Alaska and Hawaii weren't states.

- Don't turn your head every time someone says "Grandma."

It can be exhausting to try to look younger all the time, especially if you do things like running in place at the checkout counter. If you feel the symptoms of looking-younger-burnout, just relax and think of the advantages of being old:

- No one calls you lazy when you hire people to do things rather than do them yourself.

- Drivers wave you ahead in traffic and people let you step ahead of them in lines.

- You can stop struggling with contacts because glasses will cover your crow's feet and bags.

- People give you directions slowly and clearly.

- You finally have enough slips to go with every length dress.

- You don't have to run to get the phone because people let it ring longer.

- Young people's music doesn't seem as loud as it used to because you don't hear as well.

- People don't get mad anymore when you forget birthdays and anniversaries.

- You don't have to worry about dying prematurely.

If you decide your approach will be to count the blessings of maturity, be careful not to return to youth-chasing. Leather miniskirts and support hose don't go together.

Chapter 14

Beauty Is in the Eye of the Molder

Are drooping lids or wrinkled skin
Or double chins your worry?
Plastic surgery is the cure,
And you had better hurry.

Age causes the skin to sag. This is a natural process and happens to everyone. Even being rich doesn't help. In fact, the rich have more trouble with wrinkles than the rest of us because they have more time to lie in the sun getting tan, and sun worshippers soon become cosmetic-surgeon worshippers.

Naturally, you'll want to do everything you can to ward off wrinkles. Some people do this by refusing to laugh. When someone tells a joke, they say, "I already heard that one," or "I don't get it." Others think only positive thoughts so they won't frown.

Wrinkles seem to breed wrinkles, but remember that not every new line you see in the morning is a wrinkle—some are creases from the way you slept. If a line is still there eight hours later, it's a wrinkle and it's there to stay.

You can expect age to detract from beauty. To prove this to yourself, look at the picture you had taken five years ago and hated and notice how good it looks to you now.

To ease the pain of aging, learn to look for beauty in places other than your mirror. Unfortunately, you can't get away from mirrors completely. You have to look in the mirror to apply makeup and check for spinach in your teeth, and sometimes you see yourself in one accidentally. Therefore, most women consider plastic surgery at least once in their lives. One woman got so many lines from stewing about whether or not to have a face-lift that she *had* to have it.

Some people argue that having a face-lift interferes with nature. It doesn't. It's more like appealing a jail sentence you don't deserve. Or look at it this way—if you had a dress that became too loose, wouldn't you have it altered to fit?

Some women undergo cosmetic surgery when it's not warranted. Here's how to tell if it's really time to consult a plastic surgeon:

- On a windy day your skin blows in your eyes.

- A fortune teller offers to read your face.

- Customs officials check to see if you're smuggling something between the folds in your skin.

Your bathroom mirror will tell you when it's time to consult a plastic surgeon.

All older women are concerned about loosening skin. Here's what women over fifty are saying:

- "My face looks like a poorly made bed. I'd like to iron out the wrinkles."

- "I wish my mirror had a dial I could turn to eliminate the lines."

Plastic surgery is seldom covered by insurance, so you may have to postpone it until you've saved up some money. While you wait, remind yourself that wrinkles don't hurt. You can try these tricks to cover up your cosmetic problems until your knife in shining armor arrives.

- If your eyes are the problem, wear glasses with shortened bows to hold back your bagging lids.

If your chin is the problem:

- Sit on children's chairs so your knees cover it.

- Take up the violin.

- Wear flesh-colored clothing so no one can tell where your chin ends and your blouse begins.

- Hold your chin as high as possible. Pretend you're having a conversation with a giraffe, or that you're reading skywriting.

It's too bad we can't just use bobby pins to hold back our skin, but cosmetic surgeons do a wonderful job. Having to stop a man from whispering sweet nothings in your ear so he won't see the scars is a small price to pay for looking ten years younger.

Chapter 15

Don't Talk
with a Thermometer
in Your Mouth

She thinks all day about her ills
And checks the clock to take her pills.
When she's asked, "How do you feel?"
She never, ever says, "Ideal!"

Barbara Walters wrote a book called, *How to Talk with Practically Anybody about Practically Anything.* She should have added, *...Except Health.*

Once people pass their fiftieth birthday, they are ill more often, and many become obsessed with their illnesses. A woman has this addiction if she can speak clearly about an illness even though she's in a dentist's chair with the dentist's hands in her mouth. A person like this will use any excuse to talk about her health. For example, when she gives her grandchildren spelling words, she'll slip in "hypertension" and "arthritis."

Talking a lot about health can make you an unpopular person. If you don't want to lose your friends, review the list of warning signs below:

● People say "hello" but never add, "How are you?"

● You can read the doctor's writing on your prescription.

Once you pass fifty, you become obsessed with your illnesses.

- You only watch TV shows with hospital settings.

- You have to put some of your medicine in the kitchen cupboard because your medicine chest can't hold it all.

- In a restaurant, you read each menu selection aloud and explain why it would be harmful to your health.

- You have that night-before-Christmas feeling the day before your doctor's appointment.

- You research your family tree looking for illnesses you may have inherited.

If you want to be popular, guard against excessive health talk. It won't draw people to you. But if you don't get as much sympathy as you'd like, go to the greeting card section of your drug store and read the get-well messages to yourself.

Chapter 16

You on a Cold Tin Bedpan

You eat three squares (of Jell-O®)
Though it's real food you're craving.
The doctor checks your reflexes,
And says, "Your legs need shaving."

Sooner or later, most people face a hospital stay, and it's good to be prepared for it. Acceptance is the key—you have to be there, you may not leave before the doctor says you may, and you can't swap illnesses with the person in the bed next to you.

Doctors think nothing of giving you the traumatic news that you'll be entering the hospital and will no longer be in charge of your body. They say, "Let's do tests" just as if they were saying, "Let's do lunch."

Hospital nurses are extremely busy, but they're never too busy to get you out of bed and make you walk when that is the last thing in the world you want to do. You can't bribe the janitor to put a "Wet Floor" sign in front of your room so that you'll be left in bed, but you can narrate your operation to the nurse walking you so she makes the walk shorter.

You can be absolutely sure of one thing: you'll be unhappy about your appearance while you are a patient. The regulation hospital gown will make you feel terribly underdressed. But there are ways to cope:

Hospitals cost more than hotels, but they don't leave mints on your pillows.

- Try to think of your wild, matted hair as a punk hairdo.

- When visitors ask if you want anything, ask for a flattering mirror.

- Remember that a person who tells you that you look wonderful will lie about other things.

People have many different reactions to being in a hospital. The following statements are typical:

- "I want to go home so badly I would leave in the middle of 'Days of Our Lives.'"

- "I'm going to hold a wrist-band cutting ceremony when I get out of here."

- "It isn't as though I'm a rookie patient. I've watched 'Marcus Welby' and 'General Hospital' for years."

- "To me, a room with a good view is one where I can't see healthy people walking in and out of the hospital."

- "There must be an easier way to get breakfast in bed."

It's never pleasant to be a patient, but these rules can help:

- Don't tell the nurse you know a better whitener for her uniform.

- Don't feed visitors from your tray.

- Don't ask a volunteer if you can wear her smock to cover your gown's back opening.

A hospital stay may even have some advantages. Your children can't drop their kids off while they go shopping, and you don't have to wrack your brain trying to remember whether you've taken your medication.

While it is important to be a good sport about being a hospital patient, don't overdo it. You don't have to ask a nurse for the hospital's recipe for the clear beef broth, and don't feel you have to write the thank-you notes for your flowers while you are still in the recovery room.

Chapter 17

It's Just Until I Get on My Feet

It's nice to think
That "They're all grown."
But they'll move back
Or need a loan.

Just when you think your children are launched, they sail back home and drop anchor. No matter whether you've told them "Now you're on your own," or "You can always come home," the chances of their returning are the same.

You probably won't be as thrilled to have them back in the household as you were when you first brought them home from the hospital. If you're less than enthusiastic about the homecoming, just hope that your dog remembers to wag its tail and lick your child's face. In the excitement, your scowl may go unnoticed.

Since your children are afraid to simply ask, "Can I move home?" they will broach the subject indirectly. One young man said, "How'd you like to cut down on your long-distance calls?" Here are some clues that there might be a lodger in your future.

- Your son crosses out his address in your address book and doesn't write in another one.

- He asks for a house key.

Just when you think your children are launched, they sail back home and drop anchor.

- Your daughter suggests you put off selling your house.

- She has more than two suitcases when you meet her at the airport.

- He asks, "How often do you use your sewing room?"

- She was perfectly congenial on her last visit.

- He suggests you leave the extra leaf in the table.

You're bound to feel a bit uncomfortable with another person plus his or her belongings underfoot. But try to make the best of the situation:

- Be thankful you don't have to nag her about homework anymore.

- Put out guest towels for him so he'll know it's just temporary.

- Watch "Bonanza" reruns so it won't seem strange to have adult family members living with you.

- Ask your child to pay room and board. It will make the room seem more attractive and your meals more delicious.

But even though you're sorely tempted, don't make an entry in her baby book that she moved back home.

If your husband is having trouble accepting the fact that your child is moving in, you can soften the blow by making a list of various household chores he can delegate and by reminding him that you will have someone to feed the pets when you take a vacation.

Even though your child keeps assuring you that the arrangement is only temporary, watch out for signs that it isn't—such as when your son paints his name on your mailbox. When that happens it's time to threaten a move to Sun City.

Chapter 18

The Scream Heard 'Round the Block

I have a strong conviction
That a mom should be impeached
If she won't tell the sitter
The place she can be reached.

The first time you baby-sit a grandchild will be forever etched in your memory. This is the one "first" you won't want to be there for, but of course you must be.

It's been many years since your children were babies, and even more years since your high school course in infant hygiene, so it won't be easy. In fact, it could be horrible.

The worst part will be when the baby looks around for his or her parents and discovers you're supposed to take their place. There has never in history been a grandchild who smiled and waved good-bye when left with his or her grandmother for the first time.

The following things will *not* help when Baby wants Mommy:

- Saying, "Your eyes will get red and puffy if you cry."

- Taking him to your lockbox and showing him his name in your will.

- Dialing 911.

There has never been a grandchild who smiled and waved good-bye when left with his or her grandmother for the first time.

Actually, not much can be done to stop a baby from crying at this time. Just be sure your watch is waterproof. If it isn't, take it off—you can expect the tears to flow.

You'll be lucky if you don't have to baby-sit until the child is older.

Here are a few things about baby-sitting a toddler:

● You're in for a rough time if she refuses to take off her jacket and mittens.

● If you have to choose between putting a four-year-old back on the bottle or starting to smoke again, it's better to give the child the bottle.

● Don't expect to potty train him and break his thumb-sucking habit in one baby-sitting session.

● Find a toy store that delivers.

Even though the first time you baby-sit will be difficult, grandparenting is one of the brightest spots in the empty nest years. One grandmother wanted to have her driver's license picture taken with her grandchild. Another tried to get a talent scout to attend her granddaughter's school play.

Grandmothers can always explain away their grand-children's questionable behavior:

- Screaming will help their lungs grow healthy.

- Forgetting Grandma's birthday shows their sensitivity—they don't want her to feel older.

- Fighting shows they aren't wimps.

- Picking the onions out of the casserole shows they are concerned about their breath.

It's surprising that the grandparent-grandchild bond is so strong, since the former is so yesterday and the latter is so today. Think about it: your grandchild may never have seen sugar and may think you have white sand in your canister.

Chapter 19

I Love My Family, But Not Until Monday

Thanksgiving Day is fun-filled,
But there could be more delight.
If the turkey had no wishbone,
It would avoid a fight.

No self-respecting grandmother asks her children, "Why don't you and Tom come over for Thanksgiving dinner and leave the kids with a sitter?" You have to invite them all.

Thanksgiving is more work for the woman of the house than it used to be. You can't ask your daughters, daughters-in-law or granddaughters to help in the kitchen while the men watch the football game, because that would be "sexist." And no way will the men leave the game to help, so you have to do all the work yourself.

The work begins long before Thanksgiving Day. You will be cleaning, baking breads and making cucumber pickles for weeks. Then on Turkey Day, you'll look out the window and see them all piling out of the car. Tears will come to your eyes as you notice how the children have grown. The grandchild who just the other day was sitting on mail-order catalogs is now bumping his head on your chandelier.

You have an important role to play in this traditional holiday, and you must take great pains to play it well. When people ask for "just a sliver," they expect Grandma to understand that they want a huge piece.

No matter how big your family, you have to invite them all.

Follow these guidelines for a successful Thanksgiving dinner:

- Don't be a food pι sher. It isn't the end of the world if there's a bare spot on someone's plate.
- Take equal amounts from each daughter-in-law's casserole.
- Don't say, "Let Grandma hold the plate 'cuz it's heavy," to your sixteen-year-old grandson.
- Bring in clean forks for the pumpkin pie. If you leave the forks at the table, you risk stabbings between the main course and the dessert.

The Pilgrims and the Indians didn't watch a football game and let their food get cold, but that's a problem we face today. The announcer may say only four minutes remain in the game, but there should be an interpreter in the broadcasting booth to explain that that the game will be over in about an hour. Since there is no such thing as a table centerpiece with a TV screen on each side, we have to live with this plague.

Part 2
There Is Life
After Retirement

Chapter 20

In Sickness
and in Retirement

He now has time to smell the roses,
Study trees and birds in flight.
But don't you secretly desire
He do it somewhere out of sight?

As soon as your husband is home every day, you have to cook every one of his no-salt, fat-free, low-cholesterol meals. You feel like hanging a "Do Not Disturb" sign on the bathroom door and locking yourself in. You remember your first job, when your main goal was to look busy.

If your husband missed a lot of work, you'll adjust better to his retirement, but it's never easy. He's home all the time, watching you work, humming "Anything you can do, I can do better." If you had the money, you'd build another kitchen so he could have one of his own.

A wife should try to stave off her husband's retirement as long as possible. One woman was so persistent about her husband remaining on the job that during his retirement dinner she was still trying to get him to change his mind between the main course and dessert.

Probably the surest way to keep your husband working is to figure out for him when he can afford to retire in comfort. (It will probably be around the age of 110.) If that doesn't work, say, "You can't retire until you use up your business cards and wear out your business suits."

But sooner or later the day will come when he actually retires and puts you under constant surveillance. He does subtle things like duck under the telephone cord three or four times during your conversations.

You can't change the locks and keep him out of the house. After all, he worked hard all those years to support his family, and retirement is his reward. But, there's nothing wrong with planning his retirement so it won't be too hard on you.

Keeping him busy is the best alternative you have.

- Be careless with your appliances so they break and he'll have to fix them.

- Replace your "No Solicitors" sign with a sign listing his "buying hours" so he has salesmen to talk to whenever he has a spare moment.

- Ask him to make frames for all the pictures your grandchildren draw.

- Teach him any card game but bridge—you don't want him substituting in your group.

Keeping him busy at home is good, but keeping him busy away from home is even better. To achieve this:

- Remove your bird feeder and tell him to feed the pigeons in the park.

- Cancel your newspaper subscription so he'll have to buy a copy at the drug store every morning. Remind him that walking is better for the heart than driving.

- Tell everyone you meet how handy he is. Before you know it, he'll be hanging around their homes fixing things.

*A **wife** should stave off her husband's impending retirement as long as possible.*

- Get him appointed as a poll watcher on election days. Who knows—he might be inspired to run for office.

- Enroll him in a course at a community college.

- Buy your cars out of town so he has to drive there when anything goes wrong.

- Call a local concrete company to find out where they're pouring cement so he can go and watch.

Once you've found something to occupy his time, it's a good idea to prolong the deed.

- When he goes grocery shopping for you, make sure the list has at least 11 items so he can't go through the express lane.

- When you buy him a paint-by-number picture, get the one with the most numbers.

- When you serve him breakfast in bed, bring along at least two newspapers.

- When he leaves the house, tell him to drive slowly—the city is full of speed traps.

- Get him a dog with a small bladder who has to stop at every tree and fire hydrant.

Surprising as it may seem, retirement for many men is a major source of stress. Be sensitive to the change retirement has made in his life and try to cushion the shock.

You can do many things to make your husband feel as important in his retirement as he did when he was employed, such as suggesting he still wear his pager even though it will never beep:

- Make him his very own key to the bathroom.

- Suggest he sign up to be the first retired man in space.

- Install a water cooler in the kitchen.

- Type his chore list like a memo and put it in his briefcase.

- Get a picture of the person who replaced him at work and have it made into a dart board.

Retirement can be just as stressful for you as it is for him. For example, he now watches all the TV commercials, but you have less money to buy the products they advertise. Fortunately, positive thinking can make you feel better about the situation.

- Instead of thinking of your husband as your shadow, think of him as your bodyguard.

- Think how nice it is that someone's always there to say, "God bless you!" when you sneeze.

If you've been a good wife through his working years, you'll be a good wife during his retirement. You'll use the phone at the mall to complain about him, you'll resist the urge to jump on the recliner's footrest and send him flying, and you'll make sure you're not the only one crying at his retirement party.

Chapter 21

Volunteers Never Get a Company Car

Volunteer workers
Can work 'til they're tired
Without any worry
That they'll get fired.

"We've gone from two paychecks to an annual volunteer appreciation dinner," a retiree said. This is a common situation.

Although volunteering doesn't reward your hard work with money, it's much better to do something for others than to sit around the house and twiddle your thumbs—even if a certain amount of thumb-twiddling is good for arthritis. There are many needs to be met, and you'll feel good meeting a few of them. Besides, as a volunteer, you can set your own hours— or half-hours, if an hour is too much for you. After a certain age, a volunteer should be given two hours credit for every hour worked.

Leaving the business world is less of a wrench if you take up volunteer work. In fact, with a little creative thinking you'll hardly notice the change. Try these approaches:

- Talk about your volunteer work as a career change.

- Have business cards printed for your volunteer activites.

Some kids may prefer Dick and Jane to your favorite romance novel.

- Think of brown-bagging with other volunteers as a business lunch.

A few rules of decorum apply to the volunteer, and it's wise to be aware of them:

- Don't use the doctors' parking lot just because you work in the surgery waiting room.

- Don't tie the sleeves of your volunteer smock around your neck just to show off your dress.

- If you teach people to read, don't have them practice on Harlequin romance novels just because you enjoy them.

- Don't spend more than twenty minutes trying to pin your nametag on straight.

- Take your volunteer smock off occasionally so people will think you're young enough to have hot flashes.

- Even if you have lost weight, don't belt your smock to show off your waist.

- Act as if you really enjoy doing volunteer work. Don't keep asking, "What time is it?"

Even something good can be overdone. "Volunteer-aholism" is a real danger. One woman spent so much time doing volunteer work that she had to hire someone to walk her dog and water her plants.

Chapter 22

Money Matters—
It Truly Does

*When you've retired
And your income is fixed
There are hundreds of frills
That will have to be nixed.*

Just as age ranges are printed on toys so you know what to buy, income ranges should appear on other goods so retired people will know whether they could afford them.

It's important to know where you should cut corners and where you shouldn't. For example, you *should* go to the beauty parlor—drugs for the depression caused by horrible-looking hair will cost more than a hairdo.

Here are some general rules for saving money:

- Request a doggy bag for any leftover food bigger than one inch.

- Only give your grandchildren bills bearing the pictures of well-known presidents.

- Go through the express lane exclusively so you'll limit your purchases to ten items or less.

- Only buy items with an extra price sticker—that means they've been marked down.

Flirting no longer gets you off with a warning.

- Memorize the driver's manual so you won't risk getting a ticket. You're no longer at the age where you can flirt and get off with a warning.

- Don't run a half-empty dishwasher. However, do run it once a month, even if it isn't full.

- Telephone your children when the rates are low. Don't worry about the phone waking your grandchildren, you aren't the one who will have to get them back to sleep.

- Buy the cheaper cuts of meat. Tough meat is good for your teeth.

- Take a speed-reading course to avoid library fines.

- Play croquet on your lawn. It's free and the grass will get trampled so you won't have to mow it as often.

- Don't buy an answering machine, you'll have fewer calls to return.

Wouldn't it be nice if people gave you a fixed income shower when you were ready to retire? Don't get your hopes up! You'll have to get by on your fixed income without help. Remember when you used to double the chocolate chips in your cookie recipe? People on fixed incomes cut the amount in half.

Chapter 23

When in Doubt, Throw It Out

It's time to sell your big old house—
So give up what you're able.
There's half the room at your new place,
So take a leaf—not the table.

Does your heating bill make you hysterical? Are you winded by the time you answer the phone? Do you go through more than one canister of furniture polish a week?

If the answer to these questions is yes, your house is too big. However, you can't simply sell your house and move to an apartment. There are problems.

Your children will object to the move. They'll say, "You can't sell our house!" (Why they call it "our house" is a mystery. They didn't take money from their allowances to help pay the mortgage.)

At one family reunion the children organized a protest march against their parents selling the homestead. Among the arguments their parents used to put down the uprising was that the dog wasn't getting any younger and it limped from room to room to room.

Here are a few more arguments to win your children's approval of your move:

● "I could lose a grandchild if I'm baby-sitting in a house this size."

- "They're bringing nature walks through the living room to see the spiders and cobwebs."

- "I'll make the new owners promise you can still play in the tree house whenever you want."

- "We'll get more out of our tax dollars if we hold family get-togethers in the park."

The ideal time to sell is when your children's jobs and marriages are going well and no one's asking to move home. Another good time is when all your friends in real estate have retired so you don't have to decide which friend to list it with.

Of course, you'll be traumatized by moving away from the place you've called home for so many years. If you can't bear the thought of parting with your beautiful hardwood floors, leave some wet diapers on them for a few hours.

You won't be able to squeeze everything you've housed in nine rooms into four rooms. Begin by cleaning out the attic. Don't ask your most sentimenal child for help. She'll insist that you save not only her declamatory oration, but also all the rough drafts.

To make cleaning the attic easier, try these ideas:

- Invite all your children over and let them take whatever they want. To avoid fights, don't have them all over at the same time.

- Take a box of Kleenex up into the attic with you— you're sure to shed a few tears.

- Don't save trinkets thinking your grandchildren might ask for them on scavenger hunts.

- Don't talk to your children for at least a month afterwards—they're sure to ask for something you threw away

- Instead of reminiscing about the touchdowns your son made in his football jersey, think about the injuries and throw it out.

Prospective buyers may not share your taste in decorating.

- If you're alone, don't start reading your kids' old diaries. You could have a heart attack up there and no one would find you.

Selling your house may be the hardest part of moving. The things prospective buyers say in front of you will make you want to chase them out of the house with a broom. If you've just finished decorating, they're likely to say, "Of course, we will have to paint!"

You don't want to lie to prospective buyers, but you don't want to ruin the sale either. For instance, if you're asked, "Do you have a dry basement," say, "Yes"—meaning you have no bar down there.

If the prospective buyers are young, remember that the one time young people obey the commandment, "Honor thy father and mother" is when they're buying a house. They always ask one set of parents to look at the house, and in the majority of cases the father finds a major flaw. When he does, the only way to rescue the sale is to counterattack with a creative sales pitch aimed at the prospective buyer's child. Use this surefire line: "This is the first house on Santa's route."

Chapter 24

We Can Put
a Flamingo
in the Yard

He wants to move to Florida.
You'd rather not uproot.
If he wants it bad enough,
Ask him to commute.

Many men dream of retiring to a warmer climate, so if you don't want to move, you may have to figure out how to keep your husband happy in his present surroundings.

Your first task is to think of arguments for staying put. It's likely that many of your reasons will do nothing to change his thinking. Here are some arguments against moving that didn't work—so don't try them:

- Gossip about your friends will be old before you hear it.

- You'll have to leave your beautician.

- Bright sunlight will show your wrinkles.

- The humidity will warp the plaque he received when he retired.

- He'll have to ask the neighbors to bring back the tools they borrowed.

- The snow tires will go to waste.

However, with a little thought, you can come up with some arguments that are more persuasive:

- Your grandchildren and hordes of their friends will descend on you during spring break.

- A new doctor will make him lose weight.

- It could be months before your Social Security checks catch up with you.

While he's picturing the delights of Florida, you must work on making home sweet home seem sweeter. It would be ideal if you could arrange to take a Florida vacation during a hurricane. Make the best of the cold weather by building a fire in

You'll need all your persuasive powers to keep him from moving to Florida.

the fireplace. Also, be sure you are the one who pays the fuel bills so he doesn't see them.

You can also try these suggestions:

- Tell him how handsome he looks in his wool suits and topcoat.

- Let him see how you look in a swimsuit.

- List your most obnoxious friends and tell him they'll visit you in Florida.

- Complain about the heat all summer.

- Promise to wear flannel socks to bed so your feet won't freeze him.

But whatever else you do, be sure you take your Florida friends off your Christmas card list so they won't write you about the glories of living there.

Chapter 25

Do You Have a Driving Disorder?

As you drive along the highway
In your four-door rig,
You might get more respect
In a Dolly Parton wig.

If someone leaves a bus schedule under your windshield wiper, it may be time to ask yourself if you drive as well as you used to.

It's a fact that the average older driver is slower than the average young one. Even though oldsters always arrive at their destinations on time, younger people still make jokes about their driving, and this is no fun for senior citizens. Here are some typical statements made by older drivers:

- "I have no idea why everyone else is driving so fast."

- "I don't mind being passed; it's the dirty looks I get."

- "I'm so grateful when someone lets me in ahead of them that I wave thank you for half a mile."

- "I'm sure all the truck drivers are C.B.ing to each other about me."

- "I wish they'd at least have the courtesy to honk nicely."

Of course, some seasoned motorists are stodgy and earn bad reputations. One uses a yardstick to measure the space between his bumper and a fire hydrant.

If you don't want to look like a vintage driver:

- Don't use cruise control for anything less than twenty-five miles per hour.

- Don't point to a speed limit sign to let other drivers know they're breaking the law.

- Don't roll down your window and yell, "Ha ha" when you come to a stop sign and meet a driver who passed you half an hour ago.

- Don't crochet a steering wheel cover.

- Don't pull over to the side of the road and shake out your floor mats.

Before you start saving to pay a chauffeur, try these tips:

- Put a sign in the back window that says, "This car does not pass other cars."

- Buy a sign that says, "Grandma Driving." It may make other drivers think of their own grandmothers and have kinder thoughts.

- If you buy a used car with racing stripes, have it painted.

- Make a game of being slow—count how many red, blue or black cars pass you.

Some changes automatically occur when you move into

the older-age-driver category. For instance, your designated driver will be the one who took a long nap during the party. However, some rules still apply. Don't pick up a hitchhiker, no matter how much he may look like your grandson.

You know you're getting older when your designated driver has to nap during the party.

Chapter 26

I Won't Drop Out,
But I Might Drop Off

It's okay to have a boom box
With you on the campus trail.
But at your age, remember,
Keep one hand on the rail.

College isn't just for the recent high school graduate. Many "mature" women are taking classes. Education will enrich your life, even if the only reward is being able to answer more of the questions on "Jeopardy." One problem you won't have: you won't be accused of copying from someone else's paper—everyone knows you can't see that well.

Of course, this isn't going to be like the last time you were in school. The other students now think of you as an "older person" and wonder if you'll live until finals. They may even get you a chair while you're standing in the registration line.

Your college education in later life will be quite an eye-opener. Here are a few comments made by oldsters in college:

- "Now when someone offers to carry my books, I feel old instead of sexy."

- "Sometimes I have an urge to hold the other students on my lap and read to them."

There's no reason you can't be one of the gang.

- "If one more person tells me what an inspiration I am, I'll scream."

You probably know enough not to try out for cheerleading, but there are other no-no's for the grandmother in the classroom:

- Don't use the pencil sharpener in the front of the room. It shows off arm flab.

- Don't ask for show-and-tell so you can show your grandchildren's pictures.

- Try not to yawn during class, even if it is ordinarily your nap time.

- Don't complain about today's prices when you're in the college bookstore or cafeteria.

- Don't say "Whew" when you get to the top of the stairs.

- Don't ask for a senior citizen's discount in the college cafeteria.

Even though knitting an afghan in your school colors is not the thing to do, you can still be a with-it student:

- Sit near the door so you have a better chance of making it on time to the next class.

- Always carry antacid tablets in case you're invited to go out for pizza after class.

- Carry your books in a backpack to hide osteoporosis.

By combining school field trips with senior citizens' activities, you'll be able to keep a full social calendar. And going back to school will make you feel young. Imagine saying, "I can't play cards this evening because it's a school night." And think how nice it will be to receive a report card in the mail along with your Social Security check.

Chapter 27

Don't Turn Your Sewing Room into a Computer Room Until You Take a Course

I used to think "our computer's down"
Were words of mystery.
I took a course to understand,
Now what is down is me.

Since it doesn't look like computers will go the way of hula hoops, it might be a good idea to learn something about them.

Nowadays, kids become acquainted with computers before they learn to tie their shoelaces. One grandmother said, "My granddaughter is tutoring me in computers, but we have to stop sometimes so I can take her to the potty."

Some people think that once they've signed up for a computer class it's all downhill. It's not that easy. Several oldsters made the following comments about their computer courses:

It's not easy for an "old dog" to learn a new language.

- "I started to put an 'Out of Order' sign on my computer, but the teacher said, 'The machine isn't broken—it's you.'"

- "My grandson asked me to stop calling him with questions about the computer."

- "I thought after five years of computer courses I'd be able to tackle the computer category on 'Jeopardy,' but I'm still not ready."

- "If I pass, I'll build a new wing on the school."

- "I thought the teacher was making fun of my body when he said something about my floppy disk."

- "I'd like to get hold of the person who said, 'If you can type, you can work a computer.'"

- "I asked for the slowest computer they had, and I still can't catch on."

- "Is there a Heimlich maneuver to get the paper out of the printer?"

- "It should have a warning from the Surgeon General—This machine may be dangerous to your mental health."

Learning about computers may be good for the mind, but it's not good for the ego. However, if you're tired of letting your eyes glaze over when someone talks about software, take the plunge and sign up for a computer course. Don't put it off until you learn how to work your VCR.

- If you want to feel better in your computer course:

- Sign up for the class under an assumed name.

- Think of the computer as a neat pack rat.

- Pretend you have to baby-sit your grandson and bring him to class so he can translate what the teacher is saying.

- Understand that you've been disruptive if the teacher says, "Write your questions down and present the list at the end of class."

- Needlepoint a cover for your computer so the teacher can see you're good at something.

- Go home and make a never-fail recipe to restore your self-esteem.

Like everything else, computer courses involve a few no-no's.

- Don't try to block the computer screen to hide your mistakes from the teacher.

- Don't kick the computer to make it work.

- Don't be paranoid. The teacher isn't talking any slower to you than to anyone else.

- Don't think that you were put into the advanced class by mistake

There are other reasons to learn about computers besides getting a job. You'll be able to get the computer words in crossword puzzles, you'll be able to play computer games with your grandchildren, and you can be proud that you're taking your place in the modern world.

On the other hand, if you found that learning the computer was too much for you, remember: There were no computer questions in your IQ test, so evidently experts believe that computers have nothing to do with intelligence.

Chapter 28

There Isn't Room for Your Three-Wheeler in the Luggage

The bus driver's wonderful
You love him like your kin,
But don't get so enamored,
You ask him to tuck you in.

Our country is jammed with tourist attractions, and this is the time of life to take them in. That's why senior bus trips are so popular.

Taking a bus and "leaving the driving to them" has many advantages. For instance, bus drivers don't keep getting lost like husbands do. Also, when you travel with seniors exclusively, you don't risk having your seat kicked by a kid sitting behind you. Even if the older person wanted to kick, her bunions and corns would make it a no-no.

Of course, you should expect a few disadvantages from this type of touring. For instance, group snoring can be quite annoying.

To have a wonderful time on your trip, here are some suggestions:

- Be well-versed about the territory in which you're traveling. When the bus driver tells you not to drink

Taking the bus and leaving the driving to them has many advantages.

the water, you'll know whether the water is dangerous or the bus driver just doesn't want to make a restroom stop.

- Ask the bus driver if he can arrange a tour of a factory. It will make you feel good to see other people working when you are retired.

- If you fall asleep on the bus, say you were too excited about the trip to sleep the night before.

- Given a choice, ask for the older bus driver. He'll be more likely to join in on the sing-along.

A bus trip can be spoiled easily. Here are some definite "don'ts":

- Don't wake up anyone to give them a song sheet.

- Don't add facts to the bus driver's commentary.

- Don't hold up the bus while you make a phone call to the weatherline for the forecast.

- Don't bring along a space heater for your feet. Everyone will want to borrow it.

When your granddaughter talks about her senior class trip, don't start talking about your senior citizens' bus trip. She won't be thrilled having them compared.

You may have been told to bring along an empty suitcase for souvenirs, but it is best to ignore this advice. When asked for gifts you can honestly say, "I didn't have any space." And, when you're on a trip, never send letters, only postcards...so you can't send any money.

Chapter 29

Don't Put a Doily
on Top of His Stereo

When your grandson is your roomer,
You thrill to see him yawn.
You hope that he is tired
And won't stay out 'til dawn.

Teenagers are occasionally sent to live with their grandparents. Either their parents have had to move and the children don't want to, or they've become too difficult for their parents to handle.

There are advantages to having an adolescent live with grandparents instead of parents. They usually mumble. And, because your hearing is less acute, what they say won't bother you. Also, you're less likely to correct their posture because you don't want to look even shorter.

Your grandchildren were full of questions when they were little, and they still are, but now the questions all begin with "Why can't I?"

You can expect that:

- He'll look like he put himself together in less than a minute, even though he spent hours at it.

- He'll never show his anger by refusing to eat.

- Her favorite pose is standing in front of the refrigerator with the door wide open, so don't be surprised if the bulb burns out for the first time.

- The roast that used to last a week is now gone in one meal.

To minimize the cost of having a young person live with you, try these tips:

- Don't assign him too many chores. It will increase his appetite.

- Take the doodling pads away from the phone so she won't be tempted to talk even longer.

Here are some practical ideas to help you make the most of a difficult situation:

Your hearing loss may work to your advantage: what your teen-aged grandson says won't bother you.

- Sit on a telephone book at the table so he doesn't tower over you.

- Never let her select your new car. Your friends won't be able to get in and out of it.

- Start vacuuming at about the time you expect him home. You won't hear the tires squeal or the brakes screech.

- Don't make a game of seeing if she has more zits than you have wrinkles.

- Force yourself to put his picture in your *Grandma's Brag Book* album with a punk haircut, earring and all.

- Think how nice it will be if you live long enough to see him go back to his parents.

One last idea—encourage him or her to date a foreign exhange student, then fan the flames of romance. With a little luck, your grandchild might get bitten by the love bug or the travel bug, and move abroad.

Chapter 30

Take the Plastic Cover off the Loveseat

When the children all have flown,
Romance needn't leave you too—
It can be almost the same
As when you said, "I do."

For most people, raising children takes so much time and thought that they neglect romance. Now that your children are on their own and you're not distracted by "nine-to-five" jobs, you can concentrate on getting back what you had at the beginning of your marriage, when you and your husband were alone.

If you have any grandchildren, see to it that they don't beat out your husband for first place in your heart. When you display the valentines they made you, make sure his valentine is the most prominent.

It's true that age affects romance. When you try to sound breathlessly sexy on the phone, he's likely to ask, "Did you take your asthma medication today?" But with a little planning, you should do fine. Try these tips:

- Don't take a second honeymoon at Niagara Falls if you have bladder trouble.

- Don't sit in a lounge chair together—you may not be able to get out.

- Don't hold his hand too tightly. Arthritic pain detracts from romantic feelings.

You shouldn't be afraid of being too gushy. It's okay to tell him, "I love to dust because the dust rag is your old underwear."

Here are a few more romantic suggestions:

- Set out his medications so they form the shape of a heart.

- Have a heart printed between your names on your checks.

- Go to the library together and ask him to carry your books.

- Take a cruise together—or watch "Love Boat" reruns.

- Ask the orchestra leader to play "your song." (Skip this if the orchestra leader is wearing an earring—he won't know it.)

- Get matching jackets—unless you wear a bigger size.

- Spray whipped cream on his stewed prunes in the shape of a heart.

- Call him by the pet name you haven't used in forty years.

- Have a romantic dinner with foods that agree with him.

Now that your children are on their own, you can make up for lost time.

- Even though you're the only ones in the house, put a "Do Not Disturb" sign on your bedroom door.

In addition to creating romance, you also have to avoid doing things that kill romance. For example, don't be petty—if he wants to put more trash in the bag before you tie it, let him. And, never let him catch you staring at his potbelly.

The following behavior must be avoided as you attempt to cultivate romance:

- Don't doze in your chair with your head flopping and your mouth open. Go to bed at the first hint of drowsiness.

- Don't walk along the beach when the bathing beauties are out—you don't want him making comparisons.

- Don't circle advice columns that pertain to him.

- Don't get out your wedding pictures if you've gained more than fifty pounds.

- Don't go bowling if you have a big seat. There's no way you can bowl backwards.

Maybe your husband isn't the type to commission an oil painting of you, but every man has some romantic inclinations. Do things that will cause him to think of love. Here are a few ideas:

- When you pick out lingerie for your granddaughter's shower, buy something similar for yourself.

- When he's working in the basement, send your grandchild down with a love note.

- When you're on the phone, roll your eyes heavenward as though you'd much rather be talking to him.

- Put his chore list on perfumed stationery and add "I love you" at the end.

- Tweak his feet when he has them lifted for you to vacuum.

- Even if his old jokes haven't been funny in years, laugh at them.

- Take the leaves out of the table between visits from the children.

If you and your husband suffer from borderline apathy, putting the romance back into your marriage will be medicinal. Pretty soon you'll automatically take the phone off the hook before making love.

Chapter 31

We Have a Lost Husband Here

It's a major treat
When you take a trip to shop.
But bring your husband with you
And it's pretty sure to flop.

A wise shopper is one who doesn't bring her husband. Men turn into cranky little boys when they shop.

A husband never says, "That looks great on you—why don't you take it?" He says, "Couldn't you make that for half the price?" and he knows you don't sew. When you see young couples holding hands in stores, you think, "The only way he'd hold my hand would be if he were dragging me out of the mall." You can never agree on how much you should spend (and you can't show your checkbook balance to another shopper and ask her opinion).

The words you long to hear are, "Why don't we just meet back here at 2 o'clock," but he never says them. Husbands like to tag along and make life miserable for their wives. These statements were made by women whose husbands went shopping with them.

- "When I asked for his help in picking out something, he picked up a leather miniskirt."

- "I thought he was going to yawn himself to death."

Your husband won't appreciate shopping as much as you do.

- "He says that the sound of my charge card going through the machine gives him a headache."

- "When I say, 'I'll be in here just a minute' he wants to give me a lie detector test."

- "He finally handed me the car keys and took a bus home."

Since shopping is such an enjoyable part of life, look for ways to keep your husband from bugging you while you shop. Here are a few possibilities:

- Have him let you out at the door. While he's parking the car, you can have a few minutes alone.

- Shop at peak shopping times. There's a chance you'll lose him.

- Tell him to watch for shoplifters and report them. Assure him there's a reward.

- Take him to the furniture department and find him a chair in front of a television set.

If nothing you do makes him enthusiastic about shopping, be sure to remind him when you get home just how bored he was. He just might let you go shopping alone next time.

Chapter 32

Don't Chance Repeating the Vows

*Here's to fifty years
With your one and only.
Does it prove the power of love
Or the fear of alimony?*

If you stayed together for the sake of the children, it's only fair that the children pay for your fiftieth anniversary party.

Some of your children may be enthusiastic about putting on a party, but some may not. Don't let that upset you. It's very important to stay in good spirits before your fiftieth. Just the way a bride's testiness can result in a cancelled wedding, preanniversary testiness can result in divorce.

Here are a few suggestions to make your wedding anniversary a happy one:

- Try to hold your anniversary observance in the same year as a class reunion so you'll get more out of your face-lift and diet.

- Make sure your invitations are printed in large type so your friends can read them.

- Ask your maid or matron of honor to sit next to you at the head table, but not your flower girl. You won't look as good by comparison.

- Ask the newspaper not to place your picture next to a picture of a couple married for only twenty-five years.

- If your doctor attends the party, make sure people understand it's because he's a close, personal friend, not because you need him there.

- Even though your children are planning the party, it's important that you have some input. It's especially important not to let your grandchildren pick the band.

- Go to the anniversary party in the same car as your husband, no matter how you're feeling about each other.

Even if your married life is full of strife, you should declare a cease-fire for your anniversary party and observe the truce until the last guest has left. Don't pout because your husband didn't say, "Your baked beans are better than these."

Chapter 33

How to Build a Better Spouse Trap

When you held hands at twenty
You breathlessly said, "Wow!"
But holding hands at sixty
Produces just an "Ow!"

Statistics show that women live longer than men. So, there's a strong possibility that a woman will become a widow.

After she's been alone for a while, a widow may want to have a man in her life again. One woman said, "I long for a dropper and a zipper." She missed having someone drop her off at the door and zip her dress up the back.

Finding a new romance won't be easy, since widows greatly outnumber widowers. This situation cannot be improved by writing your congressman.

Nothing scares a man more than a woman who seems anxious to catch a husband, so don't sit in a bar patting the barstool beside you.

Since there are no senior singles' bars, avoid bars altogether. Instead of going barhopping at night, try restaurant-hopping in the morning. Remember that times have changed since your husband courted you. You used to toss your head back to show off your beautiful hair. Now the only reason to toss your head back is to get a pill down.

Since the number of eligible men is limited, you'll have to be creative in your efforts to meet someone.

Don't leave any stone unturned to find an eligible man.

- Buy a bumper sticker that says "Honk if you're a widower."

- When you go to senior citizens' events, write your phone number under your name on your name tag.

- Plant trees in front of your house to attract men who walk dogs. If you're really desperate, install a fire hydrant.

- When you fly, wait in the gate area to see who asks for smoking and who asks for nonsmoking before deciding whether or not you smoke.

- When you feed pigeons in the park, make sure everyone knows your crumbs are made from home-made bread.

- Volunteer to work on your class reunion committee so you can find out who's unattached.

- Hang around card shops. Older people are always buying get-well and sympathy cards.

- Get your blood pressure tested whenever there's a free check-up. You never know who you'll meet wearing a velcro arm band.

- Take your grandchildren to see Santa Claus. You have no idea who might be lurking behind that beard.

- If you place a newspaper ad for a husband, be sure it's printed in large type so it will be easier to read

If you meet someone and he asks you out to eat, try to be an exciting date. Don't have a before-dinner drink—it may make you sleepy. And don't ask the waiter to put prune juice on the menu.

If it ever gets as far as marriage, work the important things out beforehand. You'll want to know which half of the refrigerator he gets for his grandchildren's drawings and which half you get for your grandchildren's.